By day as well as night, lighthouses must be given some distinctive feature or characteristic to make them easily recognisable to the navigator for taking bearings, so they are given contrasting colours and markings to make them stand out against their backgrounds. Below, we show four alternative schemes:—

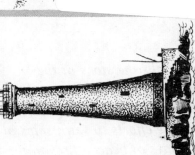

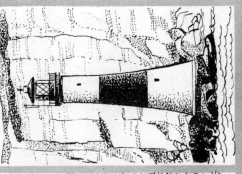

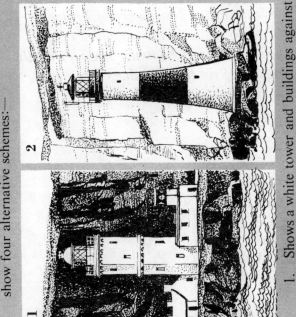

1. Shows a white tower and buildings against dark cliffs.

2. Shows a black banded tower against white cliffs.

3. Shows an all red t

4. Shows a red and white t half dark and half light background.

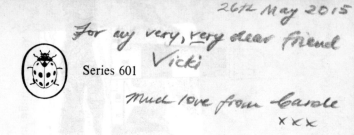

Series 601

This book tells the story of the
development of the lighthouses, lightships and
lifeboats which ensure our safety at sea. It
describes the efforts to warn ships of danger —
from the days of beacon fires to the modern
automatic lighthouse.

We learn of the importance of lightships,
and — not least — are reminded of the
courage of the lifeboatmen who voluntarily
risk their lives to help others in distress.

A LADYBIRD
ACHIEVEMENTS
BOOK
2/6 NET

A Ladybird 'Achievements' Book

The story of
LIGHTHOUSES
LIGHTSHIPS
and LIFEBOATS

by Olwen Reed

illustrations by Robert Ayton

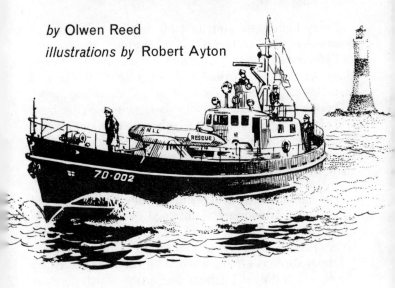

Publishers   Wills & Hepworth Ltd   Loughborough

First published 1968   ©   *Printed in England*

For the safety of ships

On all the seas of the world there are lighthouses and lightships to warn ships of danger and guide them safely on their way. Should any ship be in trouble despite these navigational aids, then there are lifeboats which can go to its aid.

Around the coasts of Britain there are about four hundred lighthouses and lightships. Most shore lighthouses can be visited up to an hour before sunset, except on Sundays or in bad weather. The lighthouse keeper on duty will show you round and explain how everything works.

Every lighthouse and lightship has its own code of flashes, so you can identify it by counting the seconds of light and darkness. If the time of darkness lasts longer than the light, it is called a 'flashing light'. If the light lasts longer than the dark, it is an 'occulting light'. Every lighthouse and lightship also has its own fog-horn code for recognition in bad weather. In daylight a lightship is identified by the name painted in huge letters on its side. Some lighthouses are painted too, usually with stripes or squares.

The lighthouses and lightships of England, Wales and the Channel Islands are maintained by the Corporation of Trinity House, founded in 1514. Scotland and Ireland have their own Lighthouse Commissioners. Lifeboat stations are maintained all round the coast by the Royal National Lifeboat Institution which depends entirely on voluntary contributions and so welcomes public interest. You may be lucky enough to look over a lifeboat or even see a practice launching.

Some of the lighthouses and lightships around our coasts

7214 0215 1

NORTH SEA

IRISH SEA

BRISTOL
CHANNEL

ENGLISH CHANNEL

The earliest beacons

When men first ventured on long sea voyages, they found that the most dangerous part often came when the journey seemed to be almost over. Many ships that had safely survived the hazards of the open sea were wrecked within sight of home. At night or in bad weather there was nothing to warn them of reefs or sandbanks, or to guide them into a safe channel.

People on shore tried to help by lighting bonfires, but a bonfire was difficult to keep alight in stormy weather, just when it was most needed. It was also too easily confused with other lights twinkling along the coast. So the habit developed of having a fire lit in the same place every night by a man whose job it was to keep it going. Then ships approaching the shore knew exactly where to look for the beacon.

Soon these fires were being lit in special braziers, called 'chauffers'. Then it was realized that the higher up they were, the further they could be seen, so before long, towers were built with the beacon fire on top.

Wood or coal fires remained popular in Northern Europe long after candles had been introduced in Mediterranean countries. Sometimes the lights were screened from wind and rain by tightly stretched hide or thin horn, but this made them hard to see. Glass panes were probably first used about 100 A.D.

Beacons warn an Elizabethan ship

The Pharos of Alexandria

The first big lighthouse in the world was built as long ago as 300 B.C. at Alexandria, a busy port with a dangerous harbour entrance. Alexander the Great, who founded the town, may have planned the lighthouse, but it was not built until the reign of Ptolemy II, son of one of Alexander's generals.

According to one description it was four hundred feet high (higher than St. Paul's Cathedral) and made of hard, white stone. The bottom section was square, then came a slightly smaller, eight-sided block and on top a round tower containing the lantern in which wood or pitch was burnt. There were many windows so that at night the light shone far out to sea, and by day the huge white building was a good landmark.

Ptolemy was determined that the lighthouse should be a lasting memorial to himself and insisted on having his name carved on it. Sostratus, the cunning Greek architect, obligingly carved the king's name in soft stone. In time this wore away and the name carved in the hard stone beneath was not Ptolemy but Sostratus.

The lighthouse became known as the Pharos, the name of the small island on which it was built. 'Phare' is still the French word for lighthouse. The Pharos was one of the wonders of the ancient world and was so strongly built that it lasted for fifteen hundred years before being destroyed by an earthquake.

The world's first big lighthouse at Alexandria

Roman lighthouses

The Romans were daring travellers as well as clever builders, so it is not surprising that they built several lighthouses. About 50 A.D. Emperor Claudius made a fine new harbour at Ostia near the capital city, Rome, and had a lighthouse with a statue of himself put on the breakwater.

Two Roman lighthouses faced each other across the English Channel at Dover and Boulogne. The one on the French coast was built by the mad emperor Caligula. In 40 A.D., at the end of a not very successful campaign, he reached the coast at Boulogne and suddenly decided to proclaim a victory over the sea. As a sign of triumph, he made his soldiers build a tower with a fire on top. It may have been a crazy idea in the first place, but it was a great help to sailors for many, many years. About eight hundred years later it was repaired on the orders of the famous French emperor Charlemagne.

In the long wars between France and England, the town of Boulogne and its lighthouse changed hands several times, being finally recaptured by the French in 1560. Elizabethan sailors affectionately called the tower the 'Old Man of Boulogne'. Although it was so useful, nobody bothered to maintain it and when, in 1644, the sea undermined the cliff on which it stood, the 'Old Man' came crashing down and .was completely destroyed.

Roman soldiers building a beacon tower

Monks, wreckers and the 'Wolf'

In the early days there were not nearly enough light-houses, so religious communities helped by keeping lights burning in dangerous areas. One was maintained by the monks of Holy Island on the Northumbrian coast. Another shone, 'like a twinkling star' according to a sixteenth century description, from the church of St. Nicholas at Ilfracombe. In Ireland the nuns of St. Anne's Convent at Youghal tended the light there for over four hundred years. In Gibraltar, captains of Spanish galleons, returning with treasure from the New World, offered gold and silver in gratitude for the light maintained in the chapel on Europa Point.

But while some people worked hard to prevent ship-wrecks, others deliberately tried to cause them. 'Wreck-ing' was a profitable source of plunder, and for hundreds of years, wreckers lured ships onto the rocks by showing false lights.

The Wolf, a treacherous rock eight miles off Land's End, is so called because at one time it had a cave in which the wind howled like a wolf. In stormy weather this warned ships to steer clear, and it is said that wreckers took a shipload of stones and blocked the hole.

After this there were many wrecks on the Wolf until a lighthouse was built by James Douglass. The men working on it often had to cling to life-lines while waves swept over them. The task took seven years and the light first shone on New Year's Day, 1870.

Wreckers carry off their booty

The first rock lighthouse

In the seventeenth century, the merchants of Plymouth felt that the Eddystone Rock was ruining their trade and needed a warning beacon. However, the Eddystone is fourteen miles out to sea and building on a wave-swept rock had never before been attempted. It seemed impossible, but an eccentric inventor called Winstanley decided to try.

He was an eccentric who lived in a house like a fun-fair, which people could visit for a shilling, and owned a show in Piccadilly called Winstanley's Waterworks. He was not a trained engineer, but he had courage and imagination.

Taking men and materials to the rock by sailing-ship was difficult, and landing was even worse. The men could only work a few hours at a time before being driven off by the rising tide. Often it was too rough to land at all. They bored twelve holes in the rock, fixed in each a long iron rod and cemented heavy granite blocks around them, Slowly a strange pagoda-like tower took shape, and the candles were first lit in 1698.

It had to be rebuilt one year later, and Winstanley boasted that his new, larger lighthouse would stand up to any weather. However, one night in November, 1703, England was struck by a storm of incredible violence. Winstanley was visiting the Eddystone, and he and his lighthouse were swept away.

Although the attempt ended in disaster, it proved that building rock lights was not impossible.

PAX
IN
BELLO

GLORY
BE TO
GOD

1698   1699

More about the Eddystone

The next Eddystone lighthouse was designed by a Cornishman, John Rudyerd who, when a small boy, ran away from home. He made his fortune and became a rich silk merchant in London. He was able to learn from Winstanley's mistakes and his lighthouse was simpler but much stronger. It was built of alternate layers of wood and stone, with an outer coat of wood.

It stood from 1706 until 1755. Then one stormy December night the lantern caught fire. The blaze spread so quickly that the three keepers barely had time to escape. On the sea-swept rock there was no shelter, but they managed to cling to the mooring rings until help arrived eight hours later.

John Smeaton, the third builder, was a brilliant engineer. His design, based on an oak tree whose spreading roots support the trunk firmly, became the accepted model for rock lights. The slim, tapering, solid-based tower, completed in 1756, was so strong that the structure was still sound one hundred and twenty years later, but it had to be replaced because the sea was undermining the rock.

James Douglass had to build the base of the fourth tower below sea-level. He first constructed a coffer-dam, a wall encircling a space from which the water is pumped. His lighthouse, which still stands, was finished in 1882. Smeaton's tower was dismantled and rebuilt on Plymouth Hoe where it can be visited.

John Rudyerd
1706

John Smeaton
1756

James Douglass
1882

EDDYSTONE
LIGHTHOUSES

70 FT

133 FT

A lighthouse on stilts

Another rock that caused many wrecks was the Smalls, twelve miles off the Pembrokeshire coast. Swift currents and fierce winds made this a dangerous area and a beacon was urgently needed.

In 1775, Henry Whiteside, a musical-instrument maker, began building a lighthouse on the almost-submerged rock. His design was a wooden, two-storeyed house supported on long oak poles embedded in the rock. Throughout the first summer the weather was so bad that work was possible on only nine whole days. The following year was better, and the lighthouse was finished in September 1776.

Keepers complained that the swaying building made them sea-sick, but it stood for eighty years, surviving many violent storms. During one of these, Whiteside was visiting his lighthouse. It was so terribly battered by huge waves that he and the keepers were desperate. They wrote three letters, put each in a bottle in a cask and threw them into the sea. One cask was washed ashore near Whiteside's home at Solva, and help soon arrived.

In 1800, one of the two keepers on duty died and the other, afraid to dispose of the body in case he was accused of murder, lived with it for two nightmare months. Since then, all rock lights have at least three keepers.

Whiteside's lighthouse was still working in 1861 when it was replaced by a more efficient tower designed by James Douglass.

A heroic deed

Grace Darling, daughter of a lighthouse keeper, spent nearly all her life in lighthouses, first on the Brownsman, an island off north-east England, then on Longstone, an even bleaker little island.

There were often wrecks on the dangerous Northumbrian coast. Twice Grace helped her father and brothers to rescue shipwrecked people from the Navestone Rock. Then, during a wild storm in September, 1838, the steamship Forfarshire struck nearby Harker's Rock and broke in two. Of the sixty-one people on board, forty-three were drowned straight away. Nine escaped in the ship's boat and the others were left clinging to the wreck. Grace's brothers were away on the mainland, so she and her father rowed their small boat through mountainous seas to rescue the survivors.

If you have ever stood on a rocky shore on a stormy night with the wind screaming and huge waves thundering, you will know how much courage and endurance were needed for this deed. Grace was not strong (she died four years later) and knew only too well the dangers of this terrible journey, but she insisted on going and so saved nine people from certain death.

Her bravery captured the public's imagination and, much against her will, Grace Darling became a national heroine.

Grace Darling and her father struggle through a raging sea

How lights developed

For hundreds of years, fires in 'chauffers' were the main beacons of Northern Europe. There was one at Tynemouth Castle as early as 1540, and there was one still in use at Saint Bees, Cumberland, in 1822. Open fires gave a good blaze to penetrate the gloom of a murky night, but used enormous amounts of wood or coal. Carrying fuel up the steep steps of a tower was hard work. For rock lights, where the landing of supplies was difficult, these wasteful fuels were out of the question.

Candles, long popular in the clearer air of Italy, were used in the first three Eddystone lighthouses. Smeaton arranged twenty-four huge candles in two circles, but in 1810 the light was converted to oil. Whiteside used oil for his 'Smalls' light.

Candles and oil lamps had to be screened from wind and rain, but windows quickly became black with soot. In 1784 the problem was solved. Ami Argand, a Swiss, invented a smokeless lamp made of two thin, brass tubes, one inside the other, with a circular wick between. He accidentally improved it when he found that the neck of a broken flask placed on top would draw up the flame and make it burn brilliantly. After this, glass chimneys were always added.

Argand lamps were widely used for lighting homes, and made possible great developments in lighthouse lights.

How lights developed : 1. An open fire. 2. Candles. 3, 4 and 5. Various types of oil lamp 6. The electric-arc light, and 7. The electric bulb

More about the development of lights

If you stand a lighted candle on a table, its rays shine all round equally, but put a mirror behind it and some of the rays are bounced forward. With a curved reflector, still more rays are collected and sent forward, giving a stronger beam. This idea was sometimes tried in early lighthouses, but the reflectors soon became caked with soot. Argand's smokeless lamp made the use of reflectors possible. The system using a curved reflector is called 'catoptric'.

In 1791 an Englishman, Thomas Rogers, tried using a lens to magnify the beam, but it was not successful. A Frenchman, Augustin Fresnel, invented a better one made from curved pieces of glass fitted over each other. One of these lenses was installed in the light at Cordouan Reef, near Bordeaux in France, in 1823. This system is called 'dioptric'. A light with both a reflector behind and a lens in front is 'catadioptric'.

In 1790 the first revolving light in the world was installed at Cordouan. This led to the invention by Englishman John Hopkinson of the group-flashing system which helps in identification. The next big advance was the use of electricity, first for shore lights, then, as the necessary apparatus became smaller, for many rock lights.

The newest development is automation. Groups of rock lights are controlled from a shore station and need only periodic checks instead of having to be permanently manned.

(above) **A modern lighting installation**
(below) **How the light is reflected and beamed**

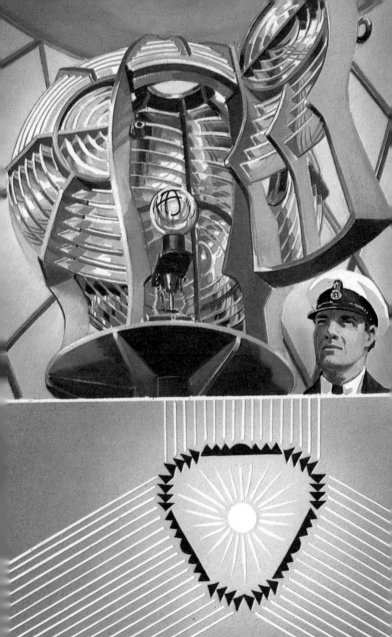

The menace of sand

Once Winstanley had shown the way, building light-houses on sea-swept rocks was often undertaken. It was never easy, but at least the builders had a solid foundation to work on. Marking sandbanks, equally dangerous to shipping, presented different problems.

Off the coast of Canada lies Sable Island, a flat, crescent-shaped island of sand barely showing above the sea. (Sable is French for sand.) There were so many wrecks on it that it was called the 'Graveyard of the Atlantic'. In 1873 two lighthouses were built, one at each tip of the crescent. The western one was built a mile inland, but gradually the sand disappeared and the sea crept nearer. In 1881 a severe storm brought it to the foot of the tower which was quickly evacuated. Before it could be dismantled, it crumbled into the sea.

In Germany, ships going to Bremerhaven were hampered by sandbanks at the mouth of the Weser. To build the Rothersand lighthouse, a caisson was floated to the spot and sunk. The bottom part was a floorless watertight chamber in which men could work on the sandy sea-bed. As sand was excavated, the caisson sank until it became firmly embedded. The hollow shell was filled with concrete, making a solid mass weighing fifty thousand tons. On this firm base a lighthouse was successfully built.

Working on the sandy sea-bed inside a caisson

A modern automatic lighthouse

The first major Trinity House lighthouse to be built for fifty years became operational in 1961. This was built at Dungeness to replace the old lighthouse, the beam of which would have been obstructed by a nuclear power station nearby.

The tower is one hundred and thirty feet high but is very slender, being only twelve feet in diameter and with walls only six inches thick. This has been made possible by the use of pre-stressed concrete. For the banding, black concrete was used in the construction, thereby ensuring that the colour remains permanent. The main machinery, stand-by generators, fog-signal equipment and electrical controls are all contained in the white base which has a spiral ramp. The operation of the light and equipment is completely automatic.

Near the top of the tower are rows of apertures in which are housed sixty loud-speaker type units which provide the electrical fog-signal, this fog-signal being automatically operated by a fog-detector—the invention of the Trinity House research staff.

The lighthouse uses an electric arc-lamp which is only slightly larger than an ordinary domestic light bulb, and which is also the result of experimental work by the Trinity House staff. It is interesting that one hundred years ago the first tests of the use of electricity for lighthouse beams were made at Dungeness, though the results obtained then were not as good as those which could be obtained at that time with the more usual oil burner.

An exciting new lighthouse

In the old days, the men who built lighthouses had a long and bitter struggle before they eventually won their battle against the fury of the sea. Their later buildings have stood the test of time and are as tough to-day as they were more than a hundred years ago, and no doubt will still be standing a hundred years hence.

The pattern of lights around our coasts has been complete for a long time, so it was exciting news to learn that the Corporation of Trinity House had decided to erect a brand new lighthouse eight miles east of Beachy Head. Replacing the 'Royal Sovereign' lightship, its cost was estimated as £500,000, twice that of a new lightship. With a crew of three, compared to the Royal Sovereign's seven, it should cost less to maintain. Also, lightships have to undergo a £12,000 refit every three years, so this new structure will prove in the long run to be cheaper and in some respects more efficient.

Work began on the new lighthouse in April 1967. It was decided to assemble the sections on the beach at Newhaven, float them on buoyancy tanks and tow them into position, ready for lowering to the sea bed where the broad base could act as a solid foundation.

All the best navigational aids that science can devise have been included in its equipment, including a two and a half million candle-power light with a forty-six mile range, a fog signal which will be heard fourteen miles off, the new Racon radar beacon and a helicopter platform.

A modern lighthouse with helicopter platform

A ship that never goes anywhere

In places where a warning beacon is needed but building one is impossible, a lightship is used. It looks like an ordinary ship with a big light, but is specially designed. Since it never has to move by itself (it is towed out to its position and anchored) it does not need a ship's usual machinery. The space so saved is taken up with generators to supply electricity for the powerful light, and compressors to provide compressed air for the fog-horn.

The master and crew of seven need comfortable living quarters and plenty of storage space for food and water supplies. They need good 'sea legs' too, as the ship rolls and pitches violently in bad weather.

Each of the thirty lightships round Britain has its own identifying signal for light and fog-horn. The light is switched on every evening before sunset, and also in fog. At first, the crew find the fog-horn deafening, but they soon get used to it. Some lightships also have a radio beacon which transmits an identification signal. This can be picked up by ships with direction-finders. On many lightships, hourly weather observations are made and passed on to the Meteorological Office for the weather reports.

Men who serve on lightships have an exacting task and deserve their generous leave—two weeks ashore after a month on duty.

The 'Bar' lightship marking the Mersey and Port of Liverpool

The notorious Goodwins

In 'wrecking' days, the Goodwin Sands off the Kent coast caused so many disasters that local boatmen were said to queue up to collect their plunder. Overseas trade had greatly increased by Queen Elizabeth I's time, and the merchants appealed to her to reduce the shipwreck risk by having a lighthouse built. A man called Gowen Smith was confident that he could reclaim the land, plant it with grass and build on it 'a fyrme and staide beacon to shewe his fyre by night'. He wanted the Treasury to give him £1,000 and the right to collect tolls from passing ships, but nobody considered the idea practicable.

It was not until 1795 that the Goodwins were lit, by one of the first lightships in the world. This reduced the danger, but even now that the area is well-lit, the Goodwins still claim victims.

On calm days at very low tide the lightship crews sometimes play cricket on the sands, but in bad weather it is a different story. The coxswain of the Walmer lifeboat once said, "Unless you have had experience of the seas on the sands, you just can't visualise with what force they can hit you." In a disastrous storm in November 1954 the South Goodwin lightship was swept away and lost with all hands.

Cricket on the Goodwin Sands

Trinity House tenders

Grocer, baker, coalman, postman, mobile library, bus, ambulance—the Trinity House tenders take the place of all these for the crews of lightships and rock lighthouses. These ships deliver food, water, fuel, mail, spare parts of machinery and anything else that is needed by the lightkeepers. They also carry the lighthouse keepers and lightship crews to and from duty, and mechanics who may be needed for special repair jobs. Sometimes they even tow the lightship itself, taking a new one to its position or removing an old one for repair or replacement.

The buoys, which mark channels, rocks and wrecks, are the responsibility of the tenders' crews, who keep them in good order. They also keep a look-out for submerged or floating wrecks and destroy them.

Sometimes the tender has to act as an ambulance, taking off a sick or injured man from the lighthouse or lightship. This is a difficult operation in rough seas. A special stretcher is used and great skill and care are necessary.

Since warning beacons are always located in areas dangerous for shipping, the little ships that service them have to be prepared for anything. Often in stormy weather it is impossible to get alongside and the 'relief' may be weeks overdue. Fortunately, vital supplies can now be delivered by helicopter, and many new and modernised lighthouses have helicopter landing platforms.

Taking off a lighthouse keeper by 'breeches buoy'

Disaster at sea

Because of technical advances there are now fewer disasters at sea, but they can still happen. Fog is one of the major causes of ships colliding or running aground: it distorts sound signals as well as reducing visibility.

Overloading made many ships founder (sink in deep water) before 1876. In that year, Samuel Plimsoll, Member of Parliament for Derby, introduced a law making a safe-loading line compulsory. This line is still known as the 'Plimsoll line'. A badly-stowed cargo can still cause a ship to break her back in heavy seas or, if it shifts, to list dangerously or even capsize.

Fire can bring disaster too, especially in cargo vessels, so strict precautions are taken. A new type of fireproof lifeboat is being developed for oil-tankers. It is completely enclosed and the roof cooled with flowing water.

Floating wrecks are another menace, and so are icebergs. In the North Atlantic the United States Coast Guard maintains a constant watch, the cost being shared by sixteen nations whose ships use these waters. The Iceberg Patrol was started after the Titanic disaster in April 1912. This splendid ocean liner on her maiden voyage struck an iceberg and sank. Because there were too few lifeboats on the ship, more than one thousand five hundred people were drowned. Since then every ship must carry enough lifeboats for everyone on board and conform to strict safety regulations.

The 'Titanic' goes down

The first lifeboats

The Crewe Trust was a legacy left by Baron Crewe, Bishop of Durham, to help victims of shipwrecks. In 1786, the Trust's chief administrator, Dr. John Sharp, heard that a London coach-builder called Lionel Lukin was experimenting with an 'unimmergible' boat with air-boxes and a cork belt. He persuaded Lukin to convert a rowing-boat for use at Bamburgh. So Grace Darling's birthplace became the first lifeboat station in the world.

Soon afterwards a Newcastle ship, the Adventure, was wrecked at the mouth of the Tyne. People on shore watched helplessly as men clinging to the rigging were washed away and drowned. They were so shocked that they offered a prize of two guineas for the best lifeboat design. Half the prize was won by William Wouldhave, parish clerk of South Shields. His design was modified and the world's first real lifeboat, the Original, was built by Henry Greathead and launched in 1790. It carried out many rescues before being wrecked forty years later. Other areas followed suit, and Greathead built more than thirty lifeboats.

William Hillary, a well-educated, much travelled man, was a member of the lifeboat crew at Douglas. In 1824 he formed the National Institution for the Preservation of Life from Shipwreck, later called the Royal National Lifeboat Institution. Another Tyne shipwreck, in 1850, stirred public feeling and made Queen Victoria interested in the Institution.

An early lifeboat

Lifeboats old and new

The first lifeboats had to be rowed. In heavy seas this was slow, dangerous and exhausting. Several designs were shown at the Great Exhibition in 1851, but there was nothing really new until about 1890 when steam was tried. This was certainly easier and quicker once the lifeboat was on its way, but it took so long to get up steam that it was not much use in an emergency.

The biggest step forward was in 1904, when a 10-horsepower petrol engine was put into a lifeboat to supplement the oars. Then bigger and more powerful engines were put in specially designed boats.

An important recent development was the introduction, in 1958, of the Oakley self-righting lifeboat which can return to normal, six seconds after capsizing. Now there is a seventy-foot lifeboat costing £57,000. It can travel six hundred and fifty nautical miles at a speed of eleven knots. It has sleeping and cooking facilities and carries, as well as the standard equipment (including searchlight, loud-hailer, breeches-buoy, parachute flares, life-jackets and axes) radar, radio telephone, Decca navigator and echo-sounder. It also carries two of the inflatable boats with outboard motors, which do such good work as inshore rescue craft.

A modern lifeboat

The courage of a lifeboat crew

One wild, windy afternoon in November 1956, the coastguard reported to the lifeboat station at St. David's, Pembrokeshire, that a French trawler was in distress six miles west of St. Ann's Head and thirteen miles from St. David's. At 4.30 p.m. the maroons were fired to summon the voluntary crew. They raced to answer the call and in thirty minutes the lifeboat was launched.

It took three hours to reach the trawler which was rolling helplessly in heavy seas. The S.S. Clair Campbell was standing by and tried to make some shelter for the lifeboat to approach the trawler. Huge waves made the ships rise and fall about twelve feet, but the coxswain managed to get close enough for two of the trawler crew to jump into the lifeboat. At the next approach the remaining six made the leap, but the lifeboat was dashed against the side of the trawler and damaged.

The night was so dark and stormy that the coxswain decided to make for Milford Haven instead of returning to St. David's. An enormous wave almost capsized the boat. One member of the crew was injured and another, 22-year-old Ieuan Bateman, was washed overboard and drowned.

After a nightmare journey the lifeboat reached Milford at 10 p.m. having saved six lives but lost one.

A smugglers' cave rescue

On an August day in 1958, two men, two girls and a fourteen-year-old boy went to explore Smugglers' Cave near Hellsmouth in Cornwall. After passing along a tunnel, they scrambled down a thirty-five foot rope into a cave partly filled by the sea. When they tried to get back, they found the rope was too damp and slippery to climb. One man who tried, fell and hurt his head. The other man decided to swim through the mouth of the cave and climb the cliff. He managed to summon help and the St. Ives lifeboat was called out.

Towing a dinghy, the lifeboat reached the cave at 7.30 p.m. Four members of the crew attempted to enter the cave in the dinghy. The little boat was tossed about on the waves and soon sank, but the men managed to swim and wade into the cave, where they found the marooned party. Now there were eight people trapped by the sea in the dark cave echoing with the thunder of crashing waves. One of the crew managed to swim out to the lifeboat. Another crew member swam back into the cave with a line, carrying a breeches-buoy for the injured man and life-jackets for the others. Everyone was hauled to the lifeboat and landed safely at St. Ives at 9.45 p.m.

Another courageous rescue

The R.N.L.I. to-day

The Royal National Lifeboat Institution has already saved about eighty-seven thousand lives and continues to save about one thousand every year. It is entirely voluntary. It costs about £1½ million a year to run, but gets no grant from the government. This means that instead of coming from rates and taxes which people are obliged to pay, all the money is willingly given.

Even more remarkable is the fact that the crews give their services free too. At most of the one hundred and fifty lifeboat stations maintained by the R.N.L.I. the only paid full-time member is the mechanic who sees that the lifeboat is always ready to put to sea. The other crew members are volunteers who give their time and risk their lives without being paid for it.

However well-designed a lifeboat is, there is always danger because it is most likely to be called out in stormy weather when other ships are seeking shelter. There have been many disasters. Two lifeboats that capsized with heavy loss of life were the one from Mumbles in Wales in 1947 and that from Arbroath in Scotland in 1953. Yet whenever the maroons are fired the lifeboat crews are ready to answer the call and to risk their own lives to help others in distress.

The lifeboat crew race to the rescue

The new radar beacon

In clear weather, navigating a ship in a busy estuary is a straight-forward task, during daylight or at night, but in dense fog it is a different matter. Even the invention of radio did not eliminate the risk of a collision with another vessel, but with the invention of radar, the navigator's nightmare ended.

Radar works on the echo principle. Electro-magnetic waves are transmitted with great rapidity from a revolving scanner mounted high up on the ship. These waves, travelling at one hundred and eighty-six thousand miles a second, radiate from the ship and bounce back off any solid object within range. The returning signals are made visible on a cathode ray tube in the form of an illuminated map with the receiving ship pinpointed in its centre. With this aid the navigator can safely steer through crowded waterways, no matter how bad the visibility.

However, there was one problem which still had to be solved: the lighthouses and lightships, those very necessary aids to navigation, registered on the radar screen like any other solid objects and could not be differentiated from them. The Corporation of Trinity House found the answer, and recently equipped a lighthouse in the mouth of the Humber with a special radar beacon, known as 'Racon'. This has proved very successful; the lighthouse shows up on the screen as a straight band of light pointing away from the receiving ship. 'Racon' can be seen by ships thirty miles away in any weather.

How the new radar beacon shows the position of a ship, lighthouse and surrounding objects

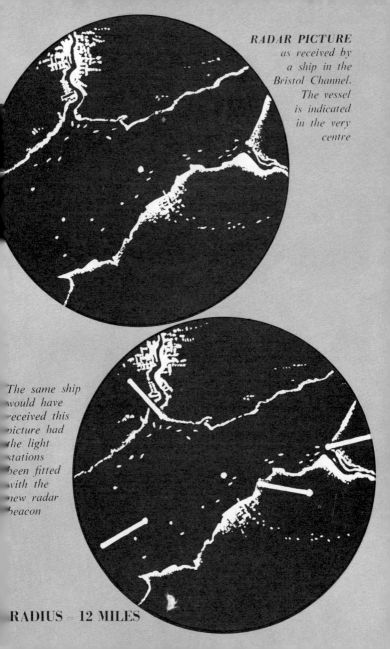

RADAR PICTURE
*as received by
a ship in the
Bristol Channel.
The vessel
is indicated
in the very
centre*

*The same ship
would have
received this
picture had
the light
stations
been fitted
with the
new radar
beacon*

RADIUS = 12 MILES

THE RNLI 70 FOOT STEEL LIFEBOAT

When necessary, this vessel can remain at sea for several days at a time and can operate in all weathers. It has a speed of 11 knots, a range of 650 miles and 150 survivors can be carried. The equipment includes the latest electronic aids and two inshore rescue boats are carried aboard.